Louisiana

by the Capstone Press
Geography Department

CAPSTONE PRESS
MANKATO, MINNESOTA

C A P S T O N E   P R E S S
818 North Willow Street • Mankato, MN 56001

Printed in the United States of America.

Library of Congress Cataloging-in-Publication Data
Louisiana/by the Capstone Press Geography Department
p. cm.--(One Nation)
Includes bibliographical references and index.
Summary: Gives an overview of the state of Louisiana, including its
history, geography, people, and living conditions.
ISBN 1-56065-442-2
1. Louisiana--Juvenile literature. [1. Louisiana.]
I. Capstone Press. Geography Dept. II. Series.
F369.3.L68 1996
975.3--dc20

96-23441
CIP
AC

Photo credits
James Rowan, cover, 5 (right), 26, 44.
Louisiana Department of Tourism, 4, 5 (left), 8.
FPG, 6.
Root Resources, 10, 22, 28, 32, 34, 37.
William Folsom, 15, 25.
Kay Shaw, 16, 18, 20, 30.

Table of Contents

Words in **boldface** type in the text are defined
in the Glossary in the back of this book.

Fast Facts about Louisiana

State Flag

Location: In the southeastern United States, on the Gulf of Mexico
Size: 51,843 square miles (134,792 square kilometers)

Population: 4,219,973 (1990 United States Census Bureau figures)
Capital: Baton Rouge
Date admitted to the Union: April 30, 1812; the 18th state

Eastern brown pelican

4

Magnolia

Largest cities:
New Orleans,
Baton Rouge,
Shreveport,
Metairie,
Lafayette,
Kenner,
Lake Charles,
Monroe,
Bossier City,
Alexandria

Nickname: The Pelican
State
State bird: Eastern
brown pelican
State flower: Magnolia
State tree: Bald cypress
State song: "Give Me
Louisiana," by
Doralice Fontane

Bald cypress

Chapter 1

Mardi Gras

People jam the sidewalks. Jazz music drifts through the air. Long parades wind through the French Quarter. They have huge floats. People on the floats wear colorful masks and costumes. They throw strands of plastic beads into the crowd. It is Mardi Gras time in New Orleans.

What Is Mardi Gras?

Mardi Gras means Fat Tuesday in French. Ash Wednesday follows Fat Tuesday. The 40 days of Lent begin on Ash Wednesday. They end on Easter Sunday. Christians give up some

Mardi Gras is a huge party held every year in New Orleans.

Gumbo is one of Louisiana's most popular foods.

foods and fun activities during Lent. Mardi Gras is their last chance to have a good time until Easter.

Mardi Gras is a huge party in New Orleans. It really starts about two weeks before Fat Tuesday. Several clubs hold daytime and evening parades. They also hold masked balls.

Other Louisiana cities celebrate Mardi Gras, too. But New Orleans holds the biggest, noisiest party of all. Thousands of visitors join in the fun each year. They eat, drink, and dance late into the night.

Other Reasons for a Visit

Louisiana is a feast of sights, sounds, and tastes. Beautiful scenery includes **bayous**, rivers, and forests. Plantation houses grace the countryside around Baton Rouge. Buildings in French and Spanish styles stand in New Orleans' French Quarter.

Many kinds of music fill Louisiana. New Orleans was the birthplace of jazz. Sometimes this music is called Dixieland. Cajun bands include accordions, fiddles, and guitars. **Zydeco** bands add washboards.

Louisiana also has great food. Pecan pies and praline candies are made with Louisiana pecans. Gumbo, jambalaya, and crawfish pies use Louisiana vegetables and shellfish.

Chapter 2
The Land

Louisiana is in the southeastern United States. It is on the Gulf of Mexico. Louisiana is known as a Gulf Coast state.

Louisiana ranks 31st in size of the 50 states. It covers 51,843 square miles (134,792 square kilometers).

All of Louisiana is lowland plains. The average **elevation** is 100 feet (30 meters) above sea level. The highest point in Louisiana is Driskill Mountain. It rises only 535 feet (161 meters) above sea level. The lowest point is in New Orleans. It is 5 feet (1.5 meters) below sea level.

All of Louisiana is lowland plains. Many fields grow rice.

Arkansas

Mississippi

Texas

Baton Rouge ★

Red River

Driskill Mountain

Mississippi River

Toledo Bend Reservoir

Pearl River

Sabine River

Atchafalava River

New Orleans

Mississippi Delta

Gulf of Mexico

The West Gulf Coastal Plain

The West Gulf Coastal Plain covers western Louisiana. It stretches from Arkansas to the Gulf of Mexico. In northern Louisiana, this land has prairies and hills.

The Kisatchie National Forest is in the north, too. Many kinds of pine trees grow there.

12

Marshy land lies south of the prairies. Cypress trees grow in these wetlands. Spanish moss hangs from their branches. Beneath this land lies rich mineral deposits. Salt, sulfur, gas, and oil are found there.

The Mississippi Plain

The Mississippi Plain covers most of eastern Louisiana. This plain gets its name from the Mississippi River. The Mississippi carries tons of **sediment** into Louisiana. The river deposits this rich soil along its banks. The river is higher than the land in some places.

The Mississippi Delta covers 13,000 square miles (33,800 square kilometers) in southeastern Louisiana. Sediment formed this land. It is the richest soil in the state.

The East Gulf Coastal Plain

The East Gulf Coastal Plain is east of the Mississippi River. It is north of Lake Pontchartrain. Low hills roll through the northern part. Marshes lie in the south.

Rivers, Lakes, and Bayous

The Mississippi River starts in Minnesota. It forms part of Louisiana's border with Mississippi. This long river then flows out of Louisiana. The Mississippi empties into the Gulf of Mexico.

The Pearl River also forms part of Louisiana's border with Mississippi. The Sabine River is to the west. It forms part of Louisiana's border with Texas. The Red, Ouachita, Atchafalaya, and Calcasieu rivers run through Louisiana.

Oxbow lakes mark where Louisiana's rivers used to flow. Other lakes were formed by dams built on rivers. Louisiana's bayous carry water that overflows from larger rivers.

Wildlife

Alligators and **nutrias** live in bayous and marshes. Otters, muskrats, and wild hogs live in wooded lowlands. Deer graze in the forests and plains of the north.

Ducks, geese, and cranes live in Louisiana. Bird-watchers may spot a brown heron or a bald eagle.

The Mississippi River forms part of Louisiana's border with Mississippi.

Climate

Warm winds blow northward from the Gulf of Mexico. These winds bring hot and humid weather in the summer. Hurricanes sometimes strike the Gulf Coast in the late summer.

Winters in Louisiana are mild and rainy. The air stays humid. The state gets almost 60 inches (152 cemtimeters) of rain every year. Louisiana is one of the wettest states.

Chapter 3

The People

About 67 percent of Louisianans are white. Many of their **ancestors** came from France, Canada, and Spain. Others came from Germany, Ireland, and Italy. Some were pioneers from neighboring southern states.

In the 1960s and 1970s, Louisiana gained almost 1 million people. Many found jobs in Louisiana's chemical plants. Others got work with the state's oil companies.

Creoles and Cajuns

Creoles are **descendants** of early French and Spanish settlers. The Creoles were Roman

Many Louisianans are Creole or Cajun.

Southern Louisiana has many Cajun towns.

Catholics. They built plantations. They started many Louisiana cities. Today, the Creoles live mainly in southern Louisiana. Many live in or near New Orleans.

The Cajuns are descendants of the Acadians. These were French people who had lived in Canada. The British forced the Acadians from Canada in the 1750s. In the 1760s, the Acadians arrived near Saint Martinville, Louisiana.

Today, Cajuns still live in southern Louisiana. Lafayette, New Iberia, and Houma have large Cajun populations. Cajun French is still spoken there. Many Cajuns make their living by fishing, trapping, or farming.

Cajuns have their own style of cooking. Jambalaya is a Cajun rice dish. It is made with shrimp, sausage, chicken, and seasonings.

African Americans

African Americans make up about 31 percent of Louisiana's population. Only Mississippi has a larger percentage of African Americans. In the 1700s, many Africans arrived in Louisiana. Plantation owners brought them to work as slaves.

Free African Americans lived there, too. Some owned their own homes and businesses. Many free African Americans lived on Isle Brevelle.

After the Civil War (1861-1865), many former slaves had their own farms. Others moved into cities to find factory jobs.

Louisiana's African Americans made important contributions to the state's cultural life. They

invented jazz in New Orleans. French-speaking African Americans created zydeco music.

Many Louisiana dishes use African foods and cooking techniques. Sweet potato dishes and gumbos are a few of them.

Native Americans

European settlers drove most Native Americans out of Louisiana. Many others died of European diseases. About 18,500 Native Americans live in Louisiana today. They are the Chitimacha, Coushatta, Houmas, and Tunica-Biloxi.

Many live on three reservations in Louisiana. The Tunica-Biloxi Reservation is near Marksville. The Coushatta Reservation is near Elton. A small Houmas fishing village stands in Dulac in Terrebonne Parish. A few Native Americans have moved into Louisiana's cities.

Asian Americans

Almost 32,000 Asian Americans live in Louisiana. More than half of their families came from Vietnam. Many of them were political **refugees**. Other Asian Americans came from China and the Philippines.

New Orleans' French Quarter is home to many people.

Chapter 4

Louisiana History

Native Americans lived in Louisiana about 12,000 years ago. They built villages along the waterways. Poverty Point, near Monroe, was an early trading center.

About 30 Native American tribes lived in Louisiana by the 1500s. They included the Attakapa, Caddo, Chitimacha, Houma, Natchez, and Tunica.

European Explorers and Settlers

Hernando de Soto was a Spanish explorer. He explored northern Louisiana in 1541. He died near Ferriday, Louisiana, in 1542.

The French arrived in 1682. Robert Cavelier, sieur de La Salle claimed all land

Baton Rouge is home to the old State Capitol Building.

drained near the Mississippi for France. He named the territory Louisiana, after King Louis XIV of France. Today's state of Louisiana is part of that land.

French settlers started Louisiana's first permanent settlement at Natchitoches in 1714. New Orleans was founded in 1718. French planters started large cotton and sugar-cane plantations. They used slaves to plant and harvest the crops. German settlers farmed the land north of New Orleans.

By 1732, the French had driven out the Natchez Indians. This opened up more land for settlement.

France gave up Louisiana to Spain in 1762. Some Spanish settlers came to the new land. In the 1760s, settlers from eastern Canada started arriving.

Statehood and War

France got Louisiana back from Spain in 1800. The United States bought Louisiana from France in 1803. Many Americans moved into Louisiana. By 1812, Louisiana had enough people to become a state.

Steamboats sail the Mississippi River to New Orleans.

New Orleans became an important trading center. Steamboats sailed down the Mississippi to New Orleans. They carried passengers, cotton, grain, and sugar cane.

In 1812, war broke out between Great Britain and the United States. The British tried to capture New Orleans in 1815. General Andrew Jackson led volunteers at the Battle of New Orleans. They defeated the British.

The Civil War and Reconstruction

Slavery divided the United States. The northern states had banned slavery. Abraham Lincoln was elected president in 1860. The southern states feared that he would end slavery. The southern states **seceded** from the United States. They formed the Confederate States of America.

The Civil War started in 1861. Louisiana sent 56,000 troops to the Confederate army. Northern ships captured New Orleans in 1862. When the South surrendered in 1865, the war ended.

After the war, all the slaves were freed. Louisiana reconstructed its government. It passed laws to protect the rights of African Americans. Louisiana became part the United States again in 1868.

Farming and New Industries

Many Louisianans became **sharecroppers** after the Civil War. Rice was a big Louisiana crop in the 1880s.

The lumber industry also grew in the 1880s. Oil was discovered in Jennings in 1901. Natural

Andrew Jackson was a hero at the Battle of New Orleans.

Oil refineries started appearing after oil was found in 1901.

gas was found near Monroe in 1916. Louisianans built oil refineries and chemical plants.

The Great Depression and World War II

The entire country suffered hardships during the Great Depression (1929-1939). Huey P. Long was Louisiana's governor. He worked to improve life in Louisiana. He gave Louisana children free school books. He hired thousands of unemployed workers. They built roads and bridges throughout the state.

The United States entered World War II (1939-1945) in 1941. The war helped Louisiana's economy. Planes, tanks, and ships used Louisiana fuel. New Orleans shipyards built boats for the navy.

Civil Rights

Louisiana took away the rights of African Americans in the 1890s. African Americans worked to win back their rights in the 1950s. **Segregation** on New Orleans buses ended in 1958. **Integration** in schools started in 1960.

African Americans throughout the South won voting rights. Ernest N. Morial became the first African-American mayor of New Orleans in 1977.

Louisiana in Recent Years

Louisiana made money from oil in the 1970s. The money was used for schools and highways. Then oil prices dropped in the 1980s. Thousands of workers lost their jobs.

The state government legalized gambling in 1992. The casinos provided thousands of jobs for Louisianans. They also brought many tourists to the state.

Chapter 5

Louisiana Business

Manufacturing, mining, agriculture, and transportation are important Louisiana businesses. Service industries play a large part, too. Tourism is a large service industry.

Agriculture and Fishing

Farms in northeastern Louisiana grow large crops of cotton and soybeans. Farms in the south grow large amounts of sugar cane and rice. Corn, sweet potatoes, strawberries, and pecans are other crops.

Beef cattle and dairy cattle are raised throughout Louisiana. Ranchers raise minks and nutria for their pelts.

Tourism, including lodging at hotels, is a big business in Louisiana.

Louisiana has some of the busiest ports in the nation.

The state also has a busy fishing industry. Shrimp and oysters are caught in the Gulf of Mexico. **Aquaculture** takes place in freshwater rivers and bayous. There, catfish and crayfish are raised.

Mining and Forestry

Louisiana is a big producer of oil and natural gas. These fuels come from wells in the Gulf of Mexico. Large salt mines lie along the coast. Sulfur mines are further inland.

Pine trees grow in Louisiana's northern forests. The logs are used for raw lumber and other wood products.

Manufacturing

Louisiana chemical plants make plastics, fertilizers, paints, soaps, and medicines. Oil refineries make gasoline from oil. Food processing plants produce white sugar, canned vegetables, and milled rice.

Transportation

Laplace, Louisiana, is the busiest port in the United States. Baton Rouge, New Orleans, and Plaquemine handle tons of goods, too. They are among the 10 busiest ports in the nation. Freighters move grain, oil, and coal to and from these ports.

Service Industries

Service industries make up the largest part of Louisiana's economy. Stores, restaurants, and hotels are some service industries. They are part of tourism. Tourists spend about 5 billion in Louisiana each year.

Chapter 6

Seeing the Sights

Louisiana has something for everyone. Nature lovers take trips along its rivers and bayous. Music lovers listen to jazz, blues, Cajun, and zydeco tunes. Other visitors learn about Louisiana history.

Northern Louisiana

The Red River crosses the plains of northern Louisiana. Henry Shreve cleared the Red River for shipping in the 1830s. He founded the city of Shreveport in 1839. The city is known for the American Rose Center. About 20,000 rosebushes grow there.

Louisiana has the tallest capitol building in the nation.

Bossier City is east across the Red River. Louisiana Downs, a thoroughbred horse-racing track, is there. Monroe is farther to the east on the Ouachita River. The river and nearby lakes and bayous attract visitors. They enjoy fishing and boating.

Central Louisiana

Toledo Bend Reservoir is to the west. It forms part of Louisiana's border with Texas. This large lake was made by damming the Sabine River. Visitors hunt, fish, and boat in the area.

Natchitoches is east of Toledo Bend. It was the first permanent European settlement in the Louisiana Purchase. The Natchitoches Folk Festival is held each October. It features Louisiana music and crafts.

The Kisatchie National Forest stands east of Natchitoches. Visitors hike and camp among its pine, ash, and gum trees. Waterskiing, swimming, and boating take place at lakes in the forest.

Baton Rouge lies to the southeast on the Mississippi River. This city is the state capital. The Louisiana State **Capitol** is 34 stories high. It is the tallest state capitol in the nation.

Natchitoches was the first European permanent settlement in the territory of the Louisiana Purchase.

Southern Louisiana

The descendants of Acadian settlers live in many southern Louisiana towns. Acadian Village in Lafayette shows how early Cajuns lived. The Evangeline Oak stands in St. Martinville. This tree played a part in a Cajun love story.

Avery Island is to the south. It is not an island, though. A salt dome rises above the flat landscape.

There the McIlhenny Company makes Tabasco Sauce from red peppers.

The Intracoastal Waterway runs across southern Louisiana. It links Barataria Bay to Sabine Lake.

Grand Isle is at the entrance of Barataria Bay. Descendants from the crew of Jean Lafitte live there. He was a pirate in the early 1800s. Today, oil is pumped near Grand Isle.

Greater New Orleans

New Orleans is Louisiana's largest city. It is on the Mississippi River. Paddle-wheel boats cruise with passengers up and down the river. The Superdome is part of the city's skyline. The Sugar Bowl football game is played there on New Year's Day.

New Orleans' French Quarter has wax museums and voodoo museums. The Garden District is nearby. Many old mansions are open to visitors.

Dixieland jazz bands play in the city. The Audubon Zoo and the Aquarium of the Americas attract many visitors.

Chalmette National Historical Park is east of the city. It is the site of the Battle of New Orleans. Lake Pontchartrain is north of New Orleans. The world's longest bridge spans the lake. It is 24 miles (38 kilometers) long.

Saint Tammany Parish is north of the lake. The Tammany Trace runs through the parish. Bikers enjoy the scenery along the trace. Slidell is to the southeast. Near there, flat-bottom boats tour the Honey Island Swamp.

Louisiana Time Line

12,000 B.C.—The first Native Americans reach Louisiana.

1541—Hernando de Soto explores northern Louisiana.

1682—Robert Cavelier, sieur de La Salle claims Louisiana for France.

1714—Louisiana's first permanent European settlement is founded at Natchitoches.

1718—New Orleans is founded.

1762—France gives Louisiana to Spain.

1760s-1790—The Acadians (Cajuns) arrive from Canada and settle in the bayous of southern Louisiana.

1800—France reclaims Louisiana.

1803—The French emperor Napoleon sells the Louisiana Territory to the United States.

1812—Louisiana becomes a state.

1815—Andrew Jackson successfully leads volunteers against the British at the Battle of New Orleans.

1861—Louisiana secedes from the Union. The Civil War breaks out between the North and the South.

1865—The South surrenders and the Civil War ends.

1868—Louisiana rejoins the Union.

1882—Baton Rouge becomes the capital of Louisiana.

1901—Louisianans drill the state's first oil well.

1935—United States senator Huey Long is assassinated in Louisiana's state capitol.

1941-1945—Louisiana oil and ships help the United States win World War II.

1956—The world's longest over-water highway bridge opens over Lake Ponchartrain.

1975—The Superdome opens in New Orleans.

1984—The Louisiana Exposition, a world's fair, is held in New Orleans.

1992—Hurricane Andrew leaves 250,000 Louisianans homeless or without power and water.

Famous Louisianans

Louis Armstrong (1900-1971) Jazz trumpeter and singer; born in New Orleans.

Evelyn Ashford (1957-) Track star who won four Olympic gold medals; born in Shreveport.

Pierre Beauregard (1818-1893) Confederate general who led the bombardment of Fort Sumter, which started the Civil War; born near New Orleans.

Terry Bradshaw (1948-) Quarterback for the four-time Superbowl champion Pittsburgh Steelers; born in Shreveport.

Truman Capote (1924-1984) An author whose works include *In Cold Blood* and *Breakfast at Tiffany's*; born in New Orleans.

Van Cliburn (1934-) Classical pianist who won the first Moscow International Tchaikovsky Piano Competition; born in Shreveport.

Michael DeBakey (1908-) Surgeon who developed the first artificial heart; born in Lake Charles.

Clementine Hunter (1886-1988) Painter of African American working people; born near Cloutierville.

Mahalia Jackson (1911-1972) Gospel singer; born in New Orleans.

Jerry Lee Lewis (1935-) Rock-and-roll singer and pianist; born in Ferriday.

Huey P. Long (1893-1935) Governor of Louisiana (1928-1932) and United States senator from Louisiana from 1932 until his assassination in 1935; born near Winnfield.

Adah Isaacs Menken (1835-1868) Famous stage actress in the United States and Europe; lived outside New Orleans.

Anne Rice (1941-) Author who is known for her vampire stories; born in New Orleans.

Bill Russell (1934-) Basketball star who led the Boston Celtics to 11 national championships; born in Monroe.

Hank Williams Jr. (1949-) Country-western singer; born in Shreveport.

Glossary

ancestor—a person from whom one is
    descended, such as a grandmother or a
    great-grandfather
aquaculture—the work of raising fish or crops
    in water
bayou—a small, slow-moving river or stream
    fed by a larger river
capitol—the building in which a legislature
    meets

descendant—a person who is born after other people in a family, such as a daughter or a grandson

elevation—the height of land measured above sea level

integration—the process of bringing people of different races together

nutria—a beaverlike animal raised for its pelt

oxbow—a curving lake that once was the bed of a river

refugee—a person who leaves another country to escape danger

secede—formally withdrew from the United States

sediment—soil carried by a river

segregation—the process of keeping people from different races apart

sharecropper—a person who farms on another's land and who must give a share of the crops to the landowner

zydeco—Cajun music that features guitar, washboard, and accordion

To Learn More

De Caro, Frank A. *Folklife in Louisiana Photography*. Baton Rouge: Louisiana State University Press, 1990.

Fradin, Dennis. *Louisiana*. From Sea to Shining Sea. Chicago: Children's Press, 1995.

Kent, Deborah. *Louisiana*. America the Beautiful. Chicago: Children's Press, 1988.

LaDoux, Rita C. *Louisiana*. Hello USA. Minneapolis: Lerner Publications, 1993.

Mitchell, William R. *Classic New Orleans*. New Orleans: Martin-St. Martin, 1993.

Internet Sites

City.Net Louisiana
http://www.city.net/countires.united_states/louisiana
Travel.org Louisiana
http://ravel.org/louisian/html.
Info Louisiana
http://www.state.la.us/
Louisiana Online
http://hob.com/louisiana/

Useful Addresses

Acadian Village
200 Green Leaf Drive
Lafayette, LA 70501

Bridge City Gumbo Festival
1701 Bridge City Avenue
Bridge City, LA 70094

Kisatchie National Forest
2500 Shreveport Highway
Pineville, LA 71360

Loyd Hall Plantation
292 Loyd Bridge Road
Cheneyville, LA 71325

Swamp Monster Tours
108 Indian Village Road
Slidell, LA 70461

Index